Alberta D. Jones

NUBS ARENA

GAME GUIDE

A Player's Guide to Winning Battles, Finding Secrets, and Rising Through the Ranks

Chapter 1: Introduction to Nubs Arena

1.1 What is Nubs!: Arena?

Nubs!: Arena is a chaotic, fast-paced multiplayer arena brawler developed by *Glowfish Interactive* in collaboration with *Rangatang*. Built for competitive yet casual fun, the game combines elements of classic party brawlers with roguelite mechanics and a uniquely whimsical aesthetic. Whether you're jumping into a match with friends locally or facing off against opponents online, Nubs!: Arena delivers a frantic and endlessly replayable gameplay experience that's easy to pick up but hard to master.

A Unique Take on the Arena Brawler Genre

At its core, Nubs!: Arena pits 4 to 20 players against each other in small, hazard-filled arenas where the goal is simple: **be the last Nub standing**. Unlike traditional fighting games or shooters, this title emphasizes short, round-based gameplay that rewards quick thinking, adaptation, and creative use of the environment. Players control "Nubs"—charming, customizable characters known for their goofy movements and expressive animations.

Core Gameplay Loop

Each round begins with players dropping into a procedurally-generated or pre-designed arena filled with deadly traps, explosive hazards, and unpredictable environmental dangers. Players scramble for weapons and power-ups, ranging from conventional melee weapons to absurd choices like slapping fish or bombs on sticks. Combat is fast and physics-driven, encouraging players to use movement and terrain to their advantage.

One of the game's standout features is its **revival system**. After a player is eliminated, they return as a floating star. If they survive long enough in this form, they can re-enter the match, adding a layer of tension and second chances that keeps gameplay dynamic until the final second.

Accessibility and Depth

Nubs!: Arena is designed to be accessible for newcomers while offering deep mechanical nuance for competitive players. Basic controls are intuitive, with movement, dodge, and attack all assigned to simple inputs. However, advanced players can experiment with environmental kills, movement tech, and arena-specific tactics to outplay opponents.

The game also incorporates **roguelite elements**, allowing players to gather temporary buffs, modifiers, or gear between rounds, giving each match a sense of evolving strategy and emergent chaos.

Visual Style and Tone

Visually, Nubs!: Arena sports a vibrant, cartoonish art style that emphasizes humor and personality. Characters are expressive, the arenas are colorfully dangerous, and the sound design complements the light-hearted chaos. Despite its competitive underpinnings, the game never takes itself too seriously, making it perfect for both casual play and more serious brawls.

Community and Future Support

The developers—veterans from the *Awesomenauts* and *Trifox* teams—have signaled their intent to support the game post-launch with additional content, such as new maps, characters, game modes, and community-driven features. Its release on Steam with a "free-to-keep" window ensures a strong early player base, paving the way for tournaments, mod support, or custom matchmaking.

1.2 Game Overview and Key Features

Nubs!: Arena is an exhilarating, high-energy multiplayer brawler that blends chaotic combat, unique roguelite progression, and strategic teamwork. Developed by *Glowfish Interactive* and *Rangatang*, this game brings together players in fast-paced, hazardous arenas where they must fight to be the last one standing. Whether playing solo, in teams, or engaging in free-for-all matches, *Nubs!: Arena* provides an experience that is both accessible and deep, appealing to a wide range of players from casual fans to competitive pros.

Key Features

1. Multiplayer Mayhem

One of the key draws of *Nubs!: Arena* is its chaotic multiplayer gameplay. Players can participate in **local** and **online matches**, battling against up to 20 players at a time. The game's easy-to-learn mechanics make it perfect for quick pick-up-and-play sessions, but the depth of the arenas and character choices ensures that there is always room for mastery. Whether in **free-for-all** or **team-based** modes, the game offers a variety of playstyles that suit different strategies.

2. Dynamic and Dangerous Arenas

Arenas in *Nubs!: Arena* are more than just battlefields—they are **living environments** filled with hazards, traps, and environmental dangers. From **spikes** to **lava** and **falling platforms**, these arenas provide a variety of obstacles that players can use to their advantage or, if they're not careful, fall victim to. Each arena offers something new to learn, with **procedurally generated elements** ensuring that no two matches feel the same.

3. Roguelite Progression System

The game's **roguelite mechanics** introduce an exciting layer of strategy as players collect **buffs**, **upgrades**, and **gear** throughout a match. These modifiers, such as increased speed, stronger attacks, or better defensive capabilities, can drastically alter the flow of a game. Players can choose to **stack power-ups** for specific playstyles or try to adapt on the fly, making each round feel fresh and offering high replayability.

4. Quirky Characters and Customization

Players control characters known as **Nubs**—adorable, customizable avatars with a wide range of expressions, skins, and outfits. Each Nub can be tailored to reflect personal preferences, from their physical appearance to how they move or respond in combat. The game provides numerous customization options, such as **color changes**, **outfit unlocks**, and **cosmetic accessories**, so no two players will look the same. The ability to personalize Nubs adds a layer of fun and identity, making the gameplay even more engaging.

5. A Variety of Weapons and Power-ups

Combat in *Nubs!: Arena* is not limited to simple hand-to-hand fighting. Players can find a variety of **weapons** scattered across the arena, each with its own strengths and weaknesses. From **melee options** like **bats and hammers** to **ranged weapons** such as **crossbows** or **explosive traps**, the variety of equipment keeps each match unpredictable. Players also have access to **power-ups**, which temporarily enhance their abilities, giving them an edge in crucial moments.

6. Respawn and Revival Mechanics

One of the most exciting features in *Nubs!: Arena* is the **revival mechanic**. When a player is eliminated, they don't just sit out for the remainder of the match. Instead, they transform into a **floating star**, where they can still affect the game by helping their teammates, collecting power-ups, or preparing for their eventual respawn. The revival mechanic keeps players invested even after they've been knocked out and ensures that the action remains exciting until the final round.

7. Simple Yet Deep Combat

While the controls of *Nubs!: Arena* are easy to grasp, the combat system is full of nuance. The game emphasizes **movement**, **dodging**, and **timing** in addition to traditional attack and defense strategies. Players can master **special moves**, **counterattacks**, and **environmental interactions**, making the learning curve steep enough for advanced players to constantly improve. For those looking for a more casual experience, the game still offers plenty of options to enjoy and be competitive without mastering every detail.

8. Community Engagement and Ongoing Updates

The developers of *Nubs!: Arena* are committed to keeping the game fresh and exciting. With regular **content updates**, **patches**, and community-driven events, the game evolves alongside its fanbase. The developers have a history of listening to player feedback, and with plans for **new arenas**, **game modes**, and **character additions**, there's always something on the horizon. Additionally, **competitive tournaments** and **leaderboards** will further fuel the competitive spirit, ensuring a long-term player base.

1.3 Story and Setting

Nubs!: Arena offers a light-hearted, whimsical world where the story takes a backseat to the action, but its setting still provides plenty of charm and atmosphere to complement the gameplay. In this game, players are thrust into a fantastical universe where Nubs—quirky, animated characters—battle in dangerous arenas filled with traps, power-ups, and dynamic environmental hazards. While there is no deep, traditional narrative, the setting and lore are woven through the design of the arenas, characters, and world-building elements that make the game's universe unique.

The World of Nubs: A Playful Battleground

At the heart of *Nubs!: Arena* is an expansive world where the Nubs live, fight, and compete. This world is divided into various **arenas**, each with its own distinctive theme, hazards, and challenges. These arenas are not merely stages for combat; they are representations of the world's vibrant, chaotic nature. The game's setting can be imagined as a playful and exaggerated version of reality where absurdity reigns and the most unpredictable events occur.

1. Arenas as Characterful Locations

Each arena in *Nubs!: Arena* is designed to reflect a unique setting, often blending **fantastical elements** with **real-world inspirations**. From **lava-filled pits** and **icy caverns** to **lush forests** and **mechanical wastelands**, the arenas offer a range of environments that challenge players to adapt their strategies. The **procedurally generated arenas** ensure that no two matches feel the same, with new hazards and dangers constantly keeping players on their toes.

The arenas are designed with both aesthetic appeal and gameplay in mind. Traps, environmental elements, and hazards are all carefully integrated into the design, making the surroundings as much a part of the challenge as the players themselves.

2. The Role of Nubs in the World

The Nubs themselves are the heart of the game's universe, yet their backstory is left largely to the imagination. These playful, adorable characters are seemingly born for one purpose: to **compete**. With their variety of **expressions**, **outfits**, and customizable appearances, Nubs are as varied as the players controlling them. While the game does not delve into their origins or personal motivations, it's easy to imagine that Nubs come from a world where battles are part of their culture—an arena-driven society that thrives on friendly competition.

The Nubs' lighthearted nature and wacky designs reflect the game's tone: competitive, but fun and full of humor. Whether wielding weapons or narrowly escaping traps, these characters are always expressive, adding to the chaotic charm of the game.

The Arena: A Battleground for Glory

The central theme of *Nubs!: Arena* is competition, and the setting serves as the perfect backdrop for this chaotic gameplay. The **arenas** themselves are treated as the main stage for the Nubs' competition. These battlegrounds are located in various regions of the world, and while they don't tell a traditional story, they each hint at different parts of the game's lore.

1. Traps and Environmental Hazards

The arenas are filled with **traps** and **hazards** designed to add layers of unpredictability to every match. These elements are not just obstacles—they're part of the environment's character. From **flames** that shoot out of walls to **collapsing floors** and **swarming creatures**, the arenas are alive with danger, ensuring that every match feels fresh. Players need to learn how to use these hazards to their advantage, or avoid them at all costs, creating a dynamic layer of strategy that ties directly into the game's environment.

2. The Competitive Spirit

While the game doesn't feature an overarching story about the Nubs' origin or their ultimate goal, it does emphasize a **culture of competition**. Players are continually striving to be the last Nub standing, with each match offering both personal and team-based victory. The game's light-hearted tone hints that, in this world, battle isn't about survival—it's about **glory**, **fun**, and **bragging rights**. This competitive drive is reflected not just in the gameplay but in the **lively atmosphere** of the arenas, where every battle is a chance to prove oneself.

A Universe Built for Chaos

The overall setting of *Nubs!: Arena* can be likened to a **competitive playground**—an arena-driven universe where anything can happen and the boundaries of reality are stretched for entertainment. There is no one singular "story" to follow; instead, the joy comes from the unpredictable, chaotic interactions between players and the environments themselves. Each match is like a mini-story of its own—one that unfolds with each twist and turn of the battle.

The game's setting also allows for expansion. As new **arenas**, **game modes**, and **characters** are introduced through updates, the world of Nubs expands in subtle ways. Players will uncover more hidden elements and Easter eggs, building a richer experience as they explore the game's evolving landscape.

1.4 Game Modes and Objectives

Nubs!: Arena offers a variety of game modes designed to keep players engaged and provide a dynamic, fast-paced experience. Each mode caters to different playstyles, from casual, fun-filled matches to more intense, competitive challenges. In all modes, the central objective is simple: **be the last Nub standing**. However, the way you achieve this varies depending on the mode, adding diversity and replayability to the game.

Core Game Modes

1. Free-for-All

The **Free-for-All** mode is the quintessential *Nubs!: Arena* experience. In this mode, players compete against each other in an all-out brawl, where the objective is to eliminate every other player while avoiding being taken out yourself. Each player fights to become the **last Nub standing** in a chaotic, constantly shifting environment. This mode is ideal for quick matches where anything can happen, making it perfect for both beginners and experienced players alike.

- **Objective**: Be the last player remaining in the arena.

- **Gameplay**: Players battle in free-for-all style with no alliances, only self-preservation. Players respawn as floating stars after elimination and can attempt to survive until re-entering the game.

- **Best For**: Quick matches, casual play, or testing out new tactics and Nubs.

2. Team Battle

In **Team Battle**, players are divided into teams, each trying to eliminate the opposing team. This mode adds a strategic layer as players must cooperate with their teammates to achieve victory. It's not just about individual skill—team coordination, timing, and tactics play an essential role in determining the winner. Team Battle also emphasizes **team-specific power-ups**, where each side might have access to unique buffs to strengthen their strategies.

- **Objective**: Eliminate the opposing team while keeping your own team alive.

- **Gameplay**: Players are divided into teams, with each team trying to outlast the other. Victory is achieved when all members of the opposing team are eliminated.

- **Best For**: Team players looking to strategize and work together, ideal for friends or organized groups.

3. Capture the Flag (CTF)

Capture the Flag (CTF) introduces an element of objective-based gameplay to *Nubs!: Arena*. In this mode, teams must attempt to steal the opposing team's flag and return it to their own base, all while defending their own flag from being captured. This mode demands strong teamwork, communication, and balance between offense and defense. It's a mode that encourages tactical planning and coordination, as players need to capture the flag without falling victim to the many hazards in the arena.

- **Objective**: Steal the opposing team's flag and return it to your base while protecting your own flag.

- **Gameplay**: The arena is divided into two sections, each containing a flag. Players must work together to breach the enemy's defenses and capture the flag while defending their own.

- **Best For**: Teams who enjoy working together to accomplish a goal and those seeking a competitive, strategic mode.

4. Roguelite Mode

For players looking for something more dynamic and unpredictable, **Roguelite Mode** offers a unique twist. In this mode, players can collect **buffs** and **power-ups** that carry over throughout a round, enabling them to evolve and adapt their playstyle as the match progresses. Players will also face a series of randomly generated obstacles and challenges within the arena, adding an element of luck and surprise. This mode encourages experimentation with different power-up combinations and tactics, offering high replayability and a fresh experience each time.

- **Objective**: Survive through multiple rounds and collect buffs to gain an edge over your opponents.

- **Gameplay**: Players battle through successive rounds, collecting upgrades and power-ups between matches. The environment is procedurally generated, ensuring no two rounds are the same.

- **Best For**: Players looking for a more varied and strategic experience, where progression and adaptability are key.

Objectives Across Modes

While the specific objectives of each mode differ, the central goal remains consistent: **become the last Nub standing**. This overarching objective emphasizes both **survival skills** and **combat prowess**, ensuring that players must continuously adapt to their surroundings, make use of the environment, and outsmart their opponents. Here's a breakdown of the general objectives in *Nubs!: Arena*:

- **Survival**: Whether it's through solo competition or team-based gameplay, staying alive is always the primary goal. Mastering movement, weapon handling, and arena navigation are essential to achieving victory.

- **Combat**: Engaging with enemies through effective use of weapons, special moves, and environmental hazards is a core component of *Nubs!: Arena*. Winning requires both offense and defense.

- **Strategic Play**: In modes like Team Battle or Roguelite, players must incorporate strategy, cooperation, and timely decision-making to achieve victory. Whether you're leading an offense, defending your team, or surviving in an ever-changing arena, strategy is key to success.

Arena-Specific Objectives

Some arenas introduce additional objectives that influence gameplay. For example, certain arenas might have areas that temporarily provide health regeneration, or others may feature intense traps that become the focal point of each match. Understanding these **environmental features** and how to use them to your advantage is crucial to mastering each arena and succeeding across different game modes.

Chapter 2: Getting Started

2.1 Installation and System Requirements

Before diving into the exciting and chaotic world of *Nubs!: Arena*, it's important to ensure that your system meets the necessary requirements to run the game smoothly. This section will guide you through the installation process and provide the minimum and recommended system specifications to help you get the most out of your experience.

Installation Process

Whether you're playing on PC, PlayStation, or other available platforms, the installation process for *Nubs!: Arena* is designed to be user-friendly and quick. Below are the steps for installing the game on various platforms.

PC (Steam)

1. **Purchase and Download**:

     ○ Head to the **Steam Store** and search for *Nubs!: Arena*.

     ○ Click on the **"Add to Cart"** button and proceed with your purchase.

     ○ Once purchased, click on the **"Library"** tab in your Steam client.

- Select *Nubs!: Arena* from your library, then click the **"Install"** button to begin the download.

2. **Installation**:

   - The game will automatically download and install once the process begins.

   - Depending on your internet connection speed, this may take anywhere from a few minutes to an hour.

   - When the installation is complete, you can launch the game directly from your Steam library.

3. **First-Time Setup**:

   - Upon launching *Nubs!: Arena* for the first time, you may need to configure your graphics settings, audio preferences, and control settings.

   - The game will typically auto-detect your system specifications and apply optimal settings, but you can manually adjust these settings in the in-game options menu.

4. **Updates and Patches**:

   - Once the game is installed, you'll be automatically notified about any available patches or updates through Steam. Keeping the game updated is important to enjoy bug fixes, performance improvements, and new features.

- Updates will automatically download and install the next time you launch the game.

PlayStation (PS4/PS5)

1. **Purchase and Download**:

   - Go to the **PlayStation Store** and search for *Nubs!: Arena*.

   - Click on the **"Buy"** option to purchase the game.

   - After purchase, the game will automatically begin downloading to your console.

2. **Installation**:

   - The game will be downloaded and installed directly onto your PlayStation system. The download time depends on your internet speed, and the game will be available to play once the installation is complete.

3. **Launch and Setup**:

   - After installation, you can find *Nubs!: Arena* in your console's main menu or library.

   - Launch the game and follow any initial setup prompts for controller configuration or preferences.

4. **Updates and Patches**:

- The PlayStation platform will handle game updates automatically when connected to the internet. You'll be prompted to download the latest updates when you start the game.

Other Platforms (Xbox, Nintendo Switch, etc.)

For Xbox, Nintendo Switch, and other platforms where *Nubs!: Arena* is available, the installation steps follow a similar pattern: purchasing the game via the respective digital store (Microsoft Store, Nintendo eShop, etc.), downloading the game, and waiting for installation to complete. Make sure you have sufficient storage space for the game, as well as a stable internet connection for smooth download and updates.

System Requirements

The system requirements for *Nubs!: Arena* vary depending on the platform you're playing on. Below, we'll provide the minimum and recommended specifications for PC users, as well as some information for console players.

PC (Steam)

To ensure optimal performance, here are the system requirements for playing *Nubs!: Arena* on a PC. These requirements allow the game to run smoothly and provide a satisfying gameplay experience.

Minimum Requirements

These are the minimum specifications needed to run *Nubs!: Arena*. You may be able to play the game with lower settings or reduced performance if your system doesn't meet these specs, but these requirements ensure that the game will run without major issues.

- **OS**: Windows 10 (64-bit)

- **Processor**: Intel Core i5-2500K / AMD Ryzen 3 1200

- **Memory**: 8 GB RAM

- **Graphics**: NVIDIA GeForce GTX 660 / AMD Radeon HD 7850

- **Storage**: 4 GB available space

- **DirectX**: Version 11

Recommended Requirements

For the best performance and to enjoy the game with higher settings, you'll want to meet or exceed the following recommended specifications. These settings provide a smoother, more visually rich experience with higher frame rates.

- **OS**: Windows 10 (64-bit)

- **Processor**: Intel Core i7-4770 / AMD Ryzen 5 2600

- **Memory**: 16 GB RAM

- **Graphics**: NVIDIA GeForce GTX 1060 / AMD Radeon RX 580

- **Storage**: 4 GB available space (SSD preferred for faster load times)

- **DirectX**: Version 11

- **Network**: Broadband internet connection (for online multiplayer)

Additional Notes

- **Controller Support**: *Nubs!: Arena* supports a wide range of controllers, including Xbox and PlayStation controllers. You can also play using a keyboard and mouse, but the controller experience tends to be more intuitive for fast-paced action.

- **Internet Connection**: A stable internet connection is required for online multiplayer matches. For the best experience, a wired connection is recommended over Wi-Fi to reduce lag and connection drops.

Console Versions (PlayStation, Xbox, Nintendo Switch)

Console players can expect the game to run optimally with no need to worry about system requirements. The game is designed to run smoothly on both current and next-gen consoles. Here's a quick guide:

- **PlayStation 4/5**: The game is fully optimized for PlayStation 4 and PlayStation 5 consoles. No specific hardware upgrades are necessary, as the game runs well across both platforms.

- **Xbox One/Xbox Series X|S**: Like the PlayStation version, *Nubs!: Arena* is fully optimized for Xbox One and Xbox Series

X|S, ensuring a seamless experience on both current and next-gen hardware.

- **Nintendo Switch**: The game runs well on the Nintendo Switch, though graphical fidelity may be slightly reduced compared to the PlayStation and Xbox versions due to the Switch's hardware limitations.

Troubleshooting and Performance Tips

- **Graphics Settings**: If your system is struggling to maintain a steady frame rate, try lowering the graphics settings. Reducing options like texture quality, anti-aliasing, and shadow quality can significantly improve performance.

- **Game Updates**: Always keep the game updated to benefit from bug fixes, performance improvements, and new features.

- **Reinstalling**: If you encounter persistent issues or bugs, reinstalling the game can often resolve many performance-related problems.

2.2 Main Menu Navigation

The main menu in *Nubs!: Arena* serves as your central hub for accessing all of the game's features, settings, and modes. Whether you're a newcomer or a seasoned player, understanding how to navigate the main menu efficiently is crucial for getting the most out of your gaming experience. In this section, we'll walk you through the layout and key options available in the main menu.

Main Menu Overview

Upon launching *Nubs!: Arena*, you'll be greeted by the main menu. This menu is designed to be intuitive and visually engaging, with easy-to-read icons and clear labels to guide you through the available options. The main menu is divided into several key sections, each offering different features and settings to customize your gameplay experience.

1. Start Game

The **Start Game** option is where you'll begin your adventure. This is where you'll access the various game modes, including Free-for-All, Team Battle, Capture the Flag, and Roguelite Mode. This section is your entry point into the action.

- **Game Mode Selection**: Once you select "Start Game," you'll be prompted to choose your preferred mode (Free-for-All, Team Battle, etc.) before jumping into a match.

- **Quick Play**: If you're looking for a fast start, you can opt for Quick Play, which will automatically match you with players in your selected mode.

2. Multiplayer

For those looking to battle it out with friends or other players online, the **Multiplayer** option is your gateway to **online gameplay**. Here, you can join public games, host private matches, or invite friends for a more personal multiplayer experience.

- **Join Match**: This will allow you to join a random multiplayer game based on your chosen mode and matchmaking preferences.

- **Create Lobby**: Create a private game lobby where you can invite friends or other players. You can customize the lobby settings such as the game mode, number of players, and arena type.

- **Friends List & Invite**: You can connect with friends who are currently playing *Nubs!: Arena* and invite them directly into your game lobby.

3. Customizations

Nubs!: Arena offers a wide range of customization options for both your character and your experience. In the **Customizations** menu, you can modify your Nub's appearance, change gameplay settings, and personalize your experience.

- **Character Customization**: Customize your Nub with different outfits, colors, and accessories. There are numerous options available to reflect your personal style and add a unique flair to your character.

- **Loadouts**: In addition to appearance, you can also customize your loadout, selecting from a variety of weapons and power-ups to tailor your playstyle.

- **Emotes & Taunts**: Show off your personality in the arenas by customizing your emotes and taunts. These can be used during the match to express yourself or taunt your opponents.

4. Settings

The **Settings** menu is where you can adjust various game options to ensure a smooth and enjoyable experience. Here, you can tweak everything from audio levels to control configurations and graphics settings.

- **Graphics Settings**: Adjust resolution, texture quality, shadow details, and frame rate options to suit your hardware and preference. These settings help you optimize the game's visual performance based on your system specifications.

- **Audio Settings**: Fine-tune sound effects, background music, and voice chat volume. You can also toggle between stereo and surround sound options to enhance the auditory experience.

- **Control Settings**: Modify key bindings (for PC players) or configure your controller settings (for console players). You can also enable or disable vibrations and adjust sensitivity for a more comfortable gameplay experience.

- **Language Options**: Select your preferred language for the game's interface, subtitles, and in-game text.

5. Store

The **Store** option gives you access to various downloadable content (DLC) and in-game purchases. Here, you can buy additional skins, emotes, weapons, or other cosmetic items that enhance your gaming experience.

- **DLC & Cosmetics**: Browse through the available DLC packs that offer new arenas, character skins, and other fun customization options.

- **Currency**: If applicable, you can purchase in-game currency here, which can be used to unlock special items, skins, and more.

6. Achievements/Trophies

In this section, you can view your progress toward unlocking **achievements** and **trophies**. *Nubs!: Arena* features a variety of goals, from completing specific challenges in-game to achieving milestones in multiplayer modes.

- **Progress Tracker**: See how far you've come in unlocking various achievements and trophies.

- **Leaderboards**: Compare your performance with other players through online leaderboards, showcasing the best players in different categories.

- **Completionist Goals**: Track your progress towards 100% completion, including hidden achievements, secret collectibles, and rare trophies.

7. Help & Support

If you're new to the game or need assistance, the **Help & Support** section is where you can find tutorials, guides, and troubleshooting information.

- **Tutorials**: Learn the basics of gameplay through the in-game tutorial that walks you through essential mechanics like movement, combat, and arena strategies.

- **Frequently Asked Questions (FAQ)**: Get answers to common queries related to gameplay mechanics, installation, and troubleshooting.

- **Technical Support**: If you encounter any issues, you can access the contact details for technical support to get help with any problems you may face, such as crashes, bugs, or connectivity issues.

Navigation Tips

- **Quick Access**: The main menu allows you to quickly access each section using the navigation bar on the left or a controller's directional pad (for console players). This makes jumping between different parts of the menu fast and intuitive.

- **Dynamic Backgrounds**: As you navigate the main menu, you'll notice dynamic background scenes that change depending on the time of day or in-game events. This adds to the immersive atmosphere of the game.

2.3 Understanding the HUD and Interface

The Heads-Up Display (HUD) and user interface (UI) in *Nubs!: Arena* are designed to provide you with essential information during gameplay, allowing you to stay informed about your character's status, objectives, and more without interrupting the action. A clear understanding of the HUD will help you make quick decisions, stay aware of your surroundings, and maximize your performance in every match.

In this section, we'll walk you through the key elements of the HUD and how to interpret the information it provides.

1. Health and Shield Bar

Located at the top-left corner of the screen, the **Health** and **Shield** bars are among the most critical elements of the HUD. These bars show your current vitality and defense levels, respectively, and are essential for determining how much damage you can take before being eliminated.

- **Health Bar**: The main bar shows your character's health. As you take damage from attacks or environmental hazards, the health bar decreases. If the health bar reaches zero, you will be eliminated from the match (in Free-for-All) or be sent to respawn (in Team Battle).

- **Shield Bar**: The shield bar, which is often represented by a secondary bar beneath your health, indicates any extra protection you have. Shields can absorb damage before health is affected. These can be replenished by picking up shield power-ups scattered throughout the arena.

2. Mini-Map

The **mini-map** is located at the top-right corner of the screen and provides a birds-eye view of the arena. This is a crucial feature for situational awareness, allowing you to track enemy positions, objectives, and environmental hazards.

- **Player Locations**: Friendly players (in Team Battle) or enemies (in Free-for-All) are marked on the mini-map, usually by icons or dots. This gives you an immediate sense of where other players are located relative to your own position.

- **Objective Markers**: In modes like Capture the Flag or specific mission-based modes, the mini-map will display objective locations. This helps you navigate toward important areas, such as the enemy flag or the location of special power-ups.

- **Environmental Hazards**: Some arenas feature traps or dangerous areas that can be marked on the mini-map, providing an early warning for when to avoid certain zones.

3. Scoreboard

The **scoreboard** is typically displayed in the top-center of the screen and gives you real-time updates on your performance as well as the progress of the entire match.

- **Player Scores**: This section shows how many eliminations (or objectives completed) each player has accumulated during the match. In Free-for-All mode, this will include individual scores, while in Team Battle, it will display team scores and individual player stats.

- **Time Remaining**: The scoreboard also includes a timer, counting down the remaining time in the match or round. This helps you strategize whether to play aggressively or defensively as time runs out.

- **Kills and Deaths**: This stat will show the number of eliminations you've made and how many times you've been eliminated during the match, providing a quick snapshot of your performance.

4. Weapon and Ammo Display

At the bottom-center of the screen, you'll find the **Weapon and Ammo Display**, which shows the weapon you are currently wielding as well as the remaining ammo.

- **Weapon Icon**: The icon for your currently equipped weapon is displayed here. You can quickly see which weapon is active and its type (melee, ranged, explosive, etc.).

- **Ammo Count**: This number indicates how many shots or uses you have left in your current weapon. If the weapon uses a specific resource (like energy or charges), it will be tracked here.

- **Weapon Switch**: On some versions of the game (such as on console), pressing a button will cycle through your available weapons, and this will update the icon and ammo count accordingly.

5. Ability and Power-Up Timer

Next to the weapon and ammo display, you'll find the **Ability and Power-Up Timer**, which tracks the cooldowns of any special abilities or power-ups you've collected.

- **Ability Icons**: Some characters in *Nubs!: Arena* have unique abilities that can be activated for a short time. These are shown as icons on this part of the HUD. The timer indicates how long until the ability is ready to use again.

- **Power-Up Timer**: In addition to character abilities, certain power-ups such as health boosts or damage amplifiers also have timers. These power-ups provide a temporary advantage, and the timer lets you know when their effect will wear off.

6. Objective Status (Mode-Specific)

Depending on the game mode, there will be different objective indicators that help guide you toward specific goals. These elements appear on the HUD to help you focus on mission objectives or the overall match goals.

- **Capture the Flag Mode**: If you're playing in a mode like Capture the Flag, the HUD will display information on your current flag status (whether you've captured it or are holding it) and the enemy flag status.

- **Team Battle Mode**: In team modes, the HUD will display the number of surviving members on each team and how many eliminations they've scored, so you can quickly assess your team's performance in comparison to the enemy's.

- **Round Timers**: In certain modes like Roguelite, where matches progress in rounds, the timer on the HUD will show how much time is left for the current round or stage.

7. Chat and Communication

For players engaging in multiplayer matches, the **chat and communication panel** appears in the lower-right corner of the screen. This section is used for team communication, enabling you to type messages to your teammates or speak via voice chat (if supported).

- **Text Chat**: Type messages to other players to communicate strategies, request assistance, or taunt your opponents.

- **Voice Chat Indicator**: If voice chat is enabled, a microphone icon will appear next to the player's name when they are speaking. This helps you quickly identify who is talking and facilitates in-game communication.

8. Exit and Pause Menu

During gameplay, you can access the **Pause Menu** by pressing the designated pause button on your controller or keyboard. This menu provides several options, such as:

- **Resume Game**: Unpauses the match and returns you to the action.

- **Settings**: Adjust in-game settings like audio, controls, or graphics.

- **Quit Match**: If you want to leave the current match early, this option allows you to exit the game mode.

2.4 First-Time Player Tips

If you're just starting out in *Nubs!: Arena*, it can be easy to feel overwhelmed by the fast-paced gameplay and diverse range of characters and modes. This section offers practical, beginner-friendly tips to help you ease into the game and start building the skills and instincts needed to compete confidently. From learning the controls to making smart tactical choices, these tips will set you on the right path.

1.1 Learn the Controls and Sensitivity Settings

Before you jump into competitive matches, take time to familiarize yourself with the game's control scheme and adjust it to your preferences.

- **Practice First**: Use the tutorial or a bot match to get comfortable with jumping, aiming, shooting, and using abilities.

- **Tweak Sensitivity**: Find a mouse/controller sensitivity that feels natural. Good aim starts with good control.

- **Master Movement Basics**: Understanding platforming elements like wall jumps, air dashes, and double jumps can help you evade attacks and chase down enemies effectively.

1.2 Choose a Beginner-Friendly Nub

Each character (Nub) comes with unique strengths, weapons, and abilities. Some are more beginner-friendly than others.

- **Start Simple**: Choose a well-rounded Nub with easy-to-use abilities and moderate speed/health.

- **Experiment Safely**: Try different characters in practice or custom matches to find one that suits your playstyle.

- **Stick With One Early On**: Focus on learning one character thoroughly before branching out to others. This helps reinforce game fundamentals.

1.3 Get Familiar with Maps and Objectives

Situational awareness often separates beginners from veterans. Knowing where you are—and where you need to be—is half the battle.

- **Study Arena Layouts**: Learn where key items spawn, such as health packs, power-ups, or weapons.

- **Watch the Mini-Map**: Use it constantly to track enemies, allies, and objectives.

- **Play the Objective**: In modes like Capture the Flag or Team Battle, prioritizing the goal over kill counts often leads to victory.

1.4 Play Smart, Not Just Fast

A reckless playstyle might net you some kills, but consistency comes from making smart decisions during combat.

- **Pick Your Battles**: Don't jump into fights where you're outnumbered. Look for lone or distracted enemies.

- **Use Terrain to Your Advantage**: Use walls, platforms, and vertical movement to outmaneuver opponents.

- **Avoid Tunnel Vision**: Don't get fixated on chasing low-health enemies—doing so can lead you into traps or dangerous territory.

Chapter 3: Gameplay Mechanics

3.1 Movement and Controls

Nubs!: Arena is built on tight, responsive movement mechanics that reward precision and creativity. Understanding how to move fluidly and take advantage of the environment is essential for survival and dominance in every match.

Movement Basics

Players can run, jump, dodge, and climb. Each Nub may have unique movement quirks, but the fundamentals are consistent across all characters. Mastering directional control, jump timing, and landing momentum will make you a harder target and a more agile attacker.

Dodging and Dashing

Dodging allows players to quickly evade incoming attacks or reposition in a tight spot. Some characters also feature directional air-dashes or evasive abilities that add vertical or lateral flexibility.

Wall Mechanics and Verticality

Many arenas feature climbable walls, ledges, and elevation changes. Wall-jumping, ledge-hanging, and bouncing off jump pads are often key to escaping danger or surprising enemies from above.

Controller vs Keyboard Layouts

The game supports both keyboard and controller inputs. Players should experiment with layouts to find what feels natural. Remapping jump, attack, and dash to comfortable positions can significantly improve reaction time and performance.

3.2 Combat System Explained

Combat in *Nubs!: Arena* is a blend of high-speed action and tactical decision-making. Each Nub comes with unique weapons or skills, making every fight unpredictable and engaging.

Attack Types

Each Nub has a primary attack and often a secondary ability or alternate fire. Some focus on ranged attacks, while others specialize in melee combat. Understanding the attack range, rate, and damage output of your chosen Nub is essential for effective play.

Knockback and Damage

As characters take damage, they become more susceptible to knockback—making it easier to launch them off the stage. Unlike traditional health bars, the game may use damage percentages or visual indicators to track vulnerability.

Special Abilities and Cooldowns

Most Nubs have special abilities with cooldowns. These include shields, dashes, traps, or ranged bursts. Smart usage of cooldowns can turn the tide in fights, especially in one-on-one engagements or team battles.

Ammo, Reloads, and Charge Systems

Some weapons require ammunition or recharging. Players must manage their resources wisely, especially during prolonged engagements where a mistimed reload could lead to defeat.

3.3 Hazards, Traps, and Arena Elements

Arenas in *Nubs!: Arena* aren't just backdrops—they're active battlegrounds filled with dangers and dynamic elements that can influence the outcome of a match.

Environmental Hazards

Spikes, lava pits, laser grids, and rotating blades can instantly damage or eliminate players. Learning hazard locations and timing is essential to avoid accidental knockouts.

Interactive Traps

Many maps feature player-activated traps—such as switches that drop platforms or set off explosions. Players who use these strategically can catch enemies off-guard or block retreat paths.

Moving Platforms and Vertical Zones

Elevators, bouncing pads, and shifting terrain require players to stay alert. Positioning near high ground or mobile elements often provides tactical advantages, especially during item or objective spawns.

Strategic Use of the Environment

Skilled players can bait enemies into hazards or use map elements to escape or flank. Every arena has hotspots—learning them offers an edge in positioning and ambush opportunities.

3.4 Respawn and Revival Mechanics

Death isn't always the end in *Nubs!: Arena*. The game includes various systems to keep players in the action, depending on the mode being played.

Respawning in Casual and Objective Modes

In non-elimination modes, players respawn after a short delay. The location may be fixed or randomized, depending on the match type, with temporary invincibility granted to prevent spawn kills.

Revival in Team-Based Modes

In certain team modes, downed allies can be revived by teammates within a time window. This adds strategic depth—do you risk reviving a teammate mid-fight, or finish off a foe first?

Elimination and Last-Nub Standing

In modes with permadeath, like Last-Nub Standing or hardcore variants, players are eliminated for the round once defeated. These matches emphasize cautious play and team coordination.

Spawn Protection and Safe Zones

To prevent unfair advantages, respawning players may be protected briefly by invulnerability or spawn zones. Smart players will use this time to reposition or regroup before reengaging.

Chapter 4: Character Roles and Classes

4.1 Overview of Nubs and Playstyles

Nubs!: Arena features a diverse cast of playable characters, each designed to cater to specific combat styles and preferences. Whether you're a fast-paced aggressor or a calculated support player, there's a Nub suited to your approach.

Combat Archetypes

Most Nubs fall into one of several archetypes—aggressors, defenders, supports, or hybrids. These archetypes influence how they behave in combat and how they interact with team dynamics.

Unique Abilities

Each Nub has a signature ability or weapon mechanic that defines their playstyle. Some offer area control tools, while others focus on high mobility or crowd control.

Difficulty and Skill Ceiling

Characters are balanced not only by power but by how difficult they are to master. Some Nubs are beginner-friendly, while others reward precision timing and advanced techniques.

Team Synergy

Some characters work best when paired with complementary Nubs. Understanding team composition is key in cooperative game modes.

4.2 Melee vs. Ranged Fighters

Combat in *Nubs!: Arena* can be categorized by attack type—primarily **melee** or **ranged**—each offering different advantages and requiring unique strategies.

Melee Fighters

Melee Nubs excel in close-quarters combat, offering high burst damage and crowd control. They often have gap-closers or dashes to help close distance quickly.

- Strengths: High damage, strong control, effective in tight spaces

- Weaknesses: Vulnerable to zoning, dependent on positioning

Ranged Fighters

Ranged Nubs specialize in keeping enemies at a distance, using projectiles or special weapons. They typically require precise aim and good awareness to avoid getting caught.

- Strengths: Safe damage output, strong in open areas, good at poking

- Weaknesses: Weaker up close, reliant on line-of-sight

Hybrid Nubs

Some characters blend both styles—using ranged attacks with melee finishers or switching between stances. These characters are versatile but often more difficult to master.

Choosing the Right Style

Player preference, map design, and enemy composition should all factor into whether a melee, ranged, or hybrid Nub is best for a given match.

4.3 Supportive and Utility Roles

Not all Nubs are designed to focus on damage. **Support** and **utility** roles play a crucial part in team success, offering healing, control, or objective-based advantages.

Buffers and Healers

These Nubs provide healing or temporary boosts to allies. Their survival is often a top priority for team-based modes.

Crowd Controllers

Some Nubs excel at disrupting enemies—slowing movement, stunning, or zoning them out of critical areas.

Objective Control Specialists

Utility-focused Nubs may have skills tailored for control-point capture, defense, or mobility, giving them a strong edge in objective-based game modes.

Defensive Abilities

From shields and barriers to traps and deterrents, support roles often offer tools that protect the team or delay the enemy's advance.

4.4 Unlocking and Customizing Nubs

Customization adds a layer of personalization to *Nubs!: Arena*, letting players tailor the experience to their liking both visually and mechanically.

Unlocking New Nubs

Nubs may be unlocked via gameplay progression, currency earned through matches, or in some cases, microtransactions. Each new Nub introduces new strategies and playstyles.

Skins and Visual Customization

Players can collect or purchase skins to change their Nub's appearance. Skins may include costumes, emotes, victory poses, and voice lines.

Loadouts and Equipment

Some Nubs may feature customizable loadouts—modifying passive traits, alternate abilities, or even weapon types depending on the game's progression system.

Progression and Mastery

Using a Nub in matches may level them up or earn cosmetic rewards. Some games also feature "Mastery Tracks" with unique challenges and unlocks for dedicated players.

Chapter 5: Weapons and Equipment

5.1 Weapon Categories and Their Uses

Weapons in *Nubs!: Arena* are diverse and tailored to suit various playstyles. While some Nubs come equipped with unique weapons, most arenas also contain pickups that can turn the tide of battle.

Melee Weapons

These include swords, hammers, axes, and energy blades. Melee weapons offer high damage up close and can stagger or knock back opponents.

- Best used by aggressive, close-range characters or when closing in for a finisher.

- Some melee weapons have arc attacks or charged slams for crowd control.

Ranged Weapons

From blasters and bows to rocket launchers and beam rifles, ranged weapons allow for safer engagements from a distance.

- Good for zoning enemies, softening targets, or defending objectives.

- Often balanced with cooldowns, reloads, or limited ammo.

Explosive and Area Weapons

Grenades, mines, or flame throwers fall into this category. They offer area-of-effect (AoE) damage and are excellent for disrupting groups or controlling choke points.

- Useful in team fights or when enemies are clustered together.

- Timing and placement are key for effectiveness.

Special Weapons

Rare or arena-exclusive weapons that grant temporary advantages, like a one-shot cannon, boomerang blade, or drone launcher.

- Usually time-limited or with restricted use.

- Can shift momentum quickly if picked up at the right time.

5.2 Item Pickups and Power-Ups

Scattered throughout the arenas are items and power-ups that offer temporary boosts or gear. Knowing what they do—and when to grab them—is a key part of gameplay.

Health Packs

Restores part of your health or shield meter. Appears in predictable spawn locations and often contested during fights.

Damage Boosts

Temporarily increases your weapon damage or attack speed. Ideal before engaging in a duel or team push.

Shield/Armor Pickups

Adds extra protection for a limited time. Especially useful for squishier Nubs or when holding an objective.

Utility Pickups

Includes speed boosts, invisibility, double jump enhancers, or cooldown reductions. These can offer unique tactical advantages, especially for flanking or escaping.

5.3 Best Loadouts for Different Scenarios

While *Nubs!: Arena* encourages experimentation, certain weapon and item combinations excel in specific game modes or team roles.

Free-For-All Loadout

Prioritize high-damage, fast-reload weapons with mobility boosts. Survivability and kill confirmation matter most here.

Objective-Based Loadout

Supportive tools like crowd control weapons, AoE traps, and healing or shield items are best suited for capture and defend scenarios.

Team Battle Loadout

A balanced mix: one main weapon (ranged or melee), one AoE or support item, and a survival-enhancing pickup like armor or speed boosts.

Duel/Tournament Loadout

Precision and timing rule here. Choose weapons with high skill ceilings and consistent damage, such as mid-range blasters or heavy melee options.

5.4 Equipment Tier List and Rarity

Not all equipment is created equal. Items and weapons often fall into rarity tiers, affecting their availability, strength, and strategic value.

Common Tier

Basic weapons or items with standard stats. Often spawn frequently and serve as reliable backups.

- Balanced and predictable, but easily outclassed by higher tiers.

Rare Tier

Slightly enhanced versions of standard gear, with improved damage, speed, or utility.

- Offer a tactical edge without overwhelming balance.

Epic Tier

High-performance gear with unique properties (e.g., bounce shots, burn damage, lifesteal).

- Usually guarded, limited-spawn, or found in the center of the arena.

Legendary Tier

Game-changing weapons or items that can dominate the battlefield for a short time.

- Risk-reward: powerful but may paint a target on your back.

- Often limited use or short duration to maintain game balance.

Chapter 6: Strategy and Tips

6.1 Beginner Tips and Common Mistakes

New players often fall into avoidable traps as they learn the game. Mastering the fundamentals early can significantly improve both survivability and performance.

Learn Your Nub First

Before diving into advanced tactics, get comfortable with one or two Nubs. Understand their movement, attacks, and cooldowns thoroughly.

Don't Button Mash

Uncontrolled spamming of attacks or abilities leaves you vulnerable. Focus on timing, spacing, and knowing when to disengage.

Watch the Edges

Environmental hazards and falling off the arena are leading causes of early knockouts. Stay centered until you're comfortable with recovery mechanics.

Prioritize Awareness

Keep an eye on your health, cooldowns, and the minimap. Tunnel visioning on a single enemy often leads to being flanked or ambushed.

6.2 Intermediate Tactics for Team Play

Once you're past the basics, teamwork becomes a core element—especially in objective-based and team elimination modes.

Role Assignment

A balanced team with clear roles (frontline, support, ranged DPS) performs better. Choose Nubs that complement your teammates rather than duplicating roles.

Communication is Key

Call out enemy positions, power-up spawns, and retreat requests. Whether using voice chat or pings, coordinated teams almost always outperform solo efforts.

Focus Fire

Team fights are won by isolating and eliminating targets quickly. Syncing attacks to burst down enemies can prevent revives and swing momentum.

Protect the Support

Healing and utility Nubs are often the backbone of a team. Assign someone to peel for them if they're under threat.

6.3 Advanced Positioning and Zone Control

At higher levels of play, victory often comes down to controlling space and denying the enemy advantageous positions.

Know the Hot Zones

Each arena has areas where fights naturally cluster—whether it's near a control point or a high-tier item spawn. Control these zones whenever possible.

Use High Ground

Vertical positioning offers better vision, safer angles, and the ability to disengage. Jump pads and wall-jumps can help reach key vantage points.

Choke Point Control

If an enemy team is funneled through a narrow passage, it's an ideal place to use AoE or traps. Anticipate their routes and set ambushes.

Don't Overextend

Chasing an enemy too far from your team can leave you isolated. Always be aware of where your allies are and whether they can support you.

6.4 Adapting Strategies for Each Arena

Every arena in *Nubs!: Arena* introduces different challenges. Adapting your approach based on the layout and environmental elements is crucial.

Small Arenas

Tight maps favor melee characters and fast-paced skirmishes. Use short-range weapons and high-mobility skills to navigate close quarters efficiently.

Vertical Arenas

Focus on characters that can double-jump, climb, or bounce. Zone denial tools like traps or mines are especially potent near ledges and platforms.

Hazard-Heavy Arenas

When traps are abundant, play with patience. Use knockback attacks to bait enemies into hazards rather than relying solely on direct damage.

Open Arenas

Long sightlines benefit ranged users. Rely on precise aim and positioning, and always watch for flanking attempts from faster Nubs.

Chapter 7: Mission and Level Walkthroughs

7.1 Arena Layouts and Stage Hazards

Each arena in *Nubs!: Arena* has a distinctive design, complete with interactive elements, environmental traps, and tactical hotspots.

Terrain Layouts

Arenas may include multiple tiers, open platforms, tight corridors, or shifting ground. Understanding each map's layout is critical for positioning, escaping, and engaging enemies effectively.

Environmental Hazards

Spikes, lava zones, rotating blades, falling platforms, and laser traps are common hazards. Most hazards can eliminate players instantly or severely injure them—so map awareness is key.

Interactive Elements

Some stages include trap switches, elevators, jump pads, destructible platforms, or dynamic zones that shift mid-match. Players who learn to control or avoid these can dramatically increase survival chances.

Spawn Zones and Objective Points

Many arenas have predictable power-up or objective spawn locations. Holding these areas can offer major strategic advantages, especially in competitive matches.

7.2 Tips for Winning in Each Arena

While general skill is vital, tailoring your strategy to each arena greatly improves your chances of winning.

Closed Arena Tips

Focus on crowd control and AoE damage. Knockback-heavy weapons are especially useful in bouncing enemies into hazards or off walls for combo finishes.

Open Arena Tips

Use ranged Nubs and keep moving to avoid becoming an easy target. Utilize line-of-sight breaks to reposition or ambush.

Vertical Arena Tips

Master movement—double-jumps, wall-slides, and upward dashes. These arenas often reward players who control the high ground.

Rotating/Changing Arenas

Stay adaptable. Some maps dynamically shift layout or hazards mid-match. Recognize warning indicators and reposition early to avoid being caught off-guard.

7.3 Multiplayer Matchflow Breakdown

Multiplayer matches in *Nubs!: Arena* follow a rhythmic structure. Understanding the tempo and flow of play helps players stay ahead.

Early Game

Focus on securing key positions and picking up early item spawns. Avoid reckless aggression—survivability and map control are more important than early eliminations.

Mid Game

Fights begin to cluster around objectives or rare item drops. Team coordination, flanking, and proper use of abilities become crucial here.

Late Game

As health pools shrink and hazards intensify, positioning and cooldown management become more impactful. This phase often determines the match outcome.

Overtime & Sudden Death

In certain modes, matches may enter a final showdown where hazards increase or respawns are disabled. Smart use of power-ups and tight formations are critical.

7.4 Roguelite Mode: Buffs and Progression Paths

The Roguelite mode offers a single-player or co-op experience where players battle through randomized stages, earn upgrades, and build powerful loadouts over time.

Stage Progression

Players advance through increasingly difficult levels, each with unique hazards, minibosses, or wave-based enemy spawns. Arena layouts may shift as the run progresses.

Buff Selection

After each stage, players can choose from a set of buffs or perks—enhancing weapon damage, cooldown reduction, mobility, or even healing effects.

- Choosing synergistic upgrades is key (e.g., pairing burn damage buffs with fire-based weapons).

- Some buffs may only be available to specific Nubs or unlocked after certain milestones.

Resource Management

Currency or tokens earned during the run can be spent on temporary items or carried over for permanent unlocks. Strategic spending influences how far players progress.

Boss Encounters

Major stages often end with unique boss fights featuring advanced AI, hazard manipulation, and multi-phase attacks. Preparation and adaptability are essential.

Chapter 8: Secrets and Collectibles

8.1 Hidden Outfits and Skins

Cosmetic customization plays a major role in player expression within *Nubs!: Arena*, and many of the coolest skins aren't available through the default store—they're hidden throughout the game.

Unlock Conditions

Some skins are earned by meeting specific criteria, such as:

- Winning a match without taking damage

- Defeating a boss using only melee attacks

- Completing all objectives in a specific arena

Exploration-Based Skins

Certain maps include breakable objects or hidden alcoves containing skin unlock tokens. Keep an eye out for subtle environmental clues.

Seasonal and Event Skins

Limited-time events often introduce exclusive cosmetics. While some return annually, others may be permanently missable after the event ends.

Secret Challenges

A few skins are tied to unlisted in-game challenges, encouraging experimentation with different Nubs, weapons, or strategies.

8.2 Easter Eggs and References

The developers of *Nubs!: Arena* have packed the game with Easter eggs—fun nods to pop culture, indie games, and even the game's own development history.

Pop Culture References

Look for items, quotes, or emotes that parody or pay tribute to famous movies, shows, or games. These are often tucked into background elements or triggered by specific actions.

Developer Cameos

Some maps feature hidden portraits, graffiti, or audio logs that reference members of the development team.

Interactive Secrets

Certain arenas have buttons or switches that, when activated in the correct sequence, trigger hidden animations or messages.

Community-Discovered Secrets

Over time, the *Nubs!* community has unearthed obscure tricks, including glitch rooms and audio tracks only accessible through unconventional gameplay methods.

8.3 Unlockable Characters and Arenas

Beyond the standard roster, additional Nubs and arenas can be unlocked through skillful play or specific achievements.

Hidden Characters

Some Nubs are unlocked by completing campaign milestones, winning a set number of online matches, or finding specific collectibles in Roguelite mode.

- Example: Unlock a stealth-based Nub by completing all arenas without being KO'd.

- Others may require earning gold medals in time trials or defeating secret bosses.

Secret Arenas

Unlisted or hidden arenas can be accessed by:

- Discovering all secrets in a specific map

- Activating hidden switches within missions

- Completing progression tracks in Roguelite mode

Alternate Game Modes

Unlocking certain Nubs or arenas may also reveal alternate versions of game modes—such as "Mirror Mode," "Gravity Shift," or ultra-hard difficulty settings.

Permanent Unlocks

Unlike temporary items, these unlocks stay with your account and may come with additional story lore or cosmetics tied to their origin.

8.4 Collectible Tracker and Completion Guide

For those aiming for 100% completion, tracking every hidden item, challenge, and unlockable is essential.

In-Game Tracker

Nubs!: Arena offers a collectible tracker accessible via the main menu. This tool shows:

- Unlocked skins, characters, and arenas

- Completed Easter egg discoveries

- Secret achievements or challenge progress

Checklist Tips

Organize collectibles by map, character, or mode. Prioritize one category at a time to avoid burn-out.

- Use community wikis or Discord servers to fill in the harder-to-find items.

- Some secrets require playing on higher difficulties or under specific conditions (e.g., with a certain loadout equipped).

Completion Rewards

Achieving 100% completion often grants unique cosmetics, a custom badge, or even a hidden cutscene. In some cases, a "true ending" is revealed in Roguelite mode once all secrets are uncovered.

Replay Value

With randomized elements and secrets tied to performance, there's plenty of incentive to replay missions while aiming for 100% mastery.

Chapter 9: Achievements and Trophies

9.1 Full List of Achievements

Nubs!: Arena includes a robust achievement system, divided into categories to reflect different aspects of gameplay.

General Achievements

- **First Blood** – Get your first KO in any mode.

- **Learning the Ropes** – Complete the tutorial.

- **Fashion Statement** – Equip a custom skin for the first time.

- **Squad Up** – Win a match in team mode.

Combat & Performance

- **Triple Threat** – Score 3 eliminations within 10 seconds.

- **Untouchable** – Win a round without taking any damage.

- **Boom Master** – KO two or more enemies with a single explosive.

- **Perfect Parry** – Block or counter three attacks in a row.

Exploration & Secrets

- **Eagle Eye** – Discover a hidden area in an arena.

- **Lore Seeker** – Unlock all developer logs or audio entries.

- **Collector Supreme** – Find all hidden cosmetics.

- **The Hidden Fifth** – Unlock a secret arena not listed in the standard pool.

Roguelite Mode

- **The Long Climb** – Reach the final boss stage.

- **Run Builder** – Equip five synergized buffs in a single run.

- **Endless Warrior** – Survive more than 30 waves.

- **One Life, One Run** – Complete the mode without dying once.

9.2 How to Unlock Rare Trophies

Some trophies are notoriously elusive and require a mix of skill, timing, and sometimes a bit of luck.

Time-Gated Events

Certain trophies are only available during seasonal events. Check the event calendar for limited-time objectives.

- **Holiday Hero** – Complete a match with a seasonal skin during an active event.

- **Egg Hunter** – Find all April Fools' Day collectibles.

Complex Multi-Phase Challenges

Examples include:

- **Flawless Victory** – Win five consecutive matches without a single KO.

- **Arena Mastery** – Get gold rankings on every arena in Score Attack mode.

- **Support Savior** – Heal teammates for a total of 10,000 HP across matches.

Community Interaction

- **Echoes of the Arena** – Share a replay with another player.

- **Trickster's Legacy** – Discover a community-created Easter egg.

9.3 Speedrunning and No-Hit Challenges

For hardcore players, *Nubs!: Arena* includes achievements designed to test the absolute limits of skill and strategy.

Speedrunning

- **Fast and Furious** – Complete Roguelite mode in under 25 minutes.

- **Any Means Necessary** – Clear five stages using only environmental hazards.

Tips:

- Use mobility-focused Nubs.

- Prioritize time-saving buffs.

- Memorize enemy spawn patterns and boss mechanics.

No-Hit Challenges

- **Shadow Walker** – Complete three missions without taking any damage.

- **Immovable Object** – Defeat a boss in Roguelite mode without losing a shield.

Recommended Strategies:

- Use ranged characters to maintain safe distance.

- Master dodging and parry mechanics.

- Equip defensive buffs early in the run.

9.4 Progress Tracking and Milestones

Keeping tabs on your achievement progress is made easy with in-game and external tools.

In-Game Tracker

- Located in the "Profile" tab.

- Displays completed achievements, trophies in progress, and percentage completion.

- Some achievements offer hints or track partial progress (e.g., "80/100 revives").

Milestone Rewards

Hitting certain achievement milestones grants in-game rewards such as:

- Special titles (e.g., "The Untouchable," "Speed Demon")

- Custom kill animations

- Alternate victory poses

- Unique lobby banners

Platform Integration

On platforms like Steam, PlayStation, and Xbox:

- Trophies sync directly with your game account.

- Some achievements unlock system-level badges or rewards (e.g., Platinum Trophy).

- Trophy rarity can be checked to see how many players worldwide have earned them.

Chapter 10: Advanced Techniques and Resources

10.1 Movement Tech and Input Optimization

Elite players rely on advanced movement mechanics and refined input setups to outmaneuver opponents and gain frame-perfect advantages.

Dash Cancelling

Some Nubs allow attacks to be canceled mid-animation with a dash, allowing fluid combos or quick disengagements. This reduces recovery frames and opens up new movement pathways.

Momentum Preservation

Jumping or dashing into slopes or moving platforms can preserve or boost momentum. Skilled players use this to extend jumps or traverse maps faster.

Wall Hops and Ledge Tricks

Certain arenas allow wall interactions that are not explicitly taught in tutorials. Wall hops—quickly bouncing between two walls—can stall for cooldowns or evade attacks. Ledge vaulting can bait opponents into overextending.

Input Customization

Customize your button layout to reduce finger strain and improve access to key abilities. Many top players bind dash or jump to bumpers/triggers for faster response times.

10.2 Hitbox Exploits and Frame Knowledge

Understanding how hitboxes and animation frames work can dramatically increase accuracy and survivability in high-stakes matches.

Active Frames vs. Recovery Frames

Each move in *Nubs!* has startup, active, and recovery phases. Knowing when your attacks are active helps time hits precisely, while understanding recovery lets you predict punish windows.

Phantom Hitboxes

Some weapons or abilities extend their hitboxes briefly beyond the animation—these are often exploitable with frame-perfect timing.

Hurtbox Shifting

Some Nubs have animation frames during movement where their hitbox shifts or shrinks. Learning these allows you to dodge through attacks with precision (akin to "I-frames" in other games).

Clash Interactions

When two attacks collide, the result depends on priority and timing. Advanced players use move priority knowledge to bait or interrupt opponents reliably.

10.3 Patch Notes and Meta Shifts

The game's meta (most effective tactics available) evolves with each balance patch, making it important to stay current.

Reading Patch Notes

Each update includes detailed breakdowns of:

- Buffs/nerfs to characters or weapons

- Arena modifications

- System-level changes (e.g., knockback physics, cooldown scaling)

Understanding these lets players adapt their strategies or loadouts before competitive matches.

Tier Shifts

Post-patch, the tier list may shift. A Nub considered weak may become top-tier after buffs, or dominant picks may receive nerfs that open up new playstyles.

Experimental Changes

Some patches introduce limited-time mechanics or "testbed" adjustments. Participating in these helps influence future balance decisions while giving early insight into potential meta shifts.

10.4 Community Resources and Competitive Scene

The *Nubs!: Arena* community is vibrant and filled with tools to help you improve, connect, and compete.

Official and Fan Resources

- **Discord Servers** – Strategy discussion, LFG, developer Q&A

- **Wikis & Guides** – Frame data, arena maps, combo routes

- **YouTube/Twitch** – High-level play breakdowns, tutorials, and tournament VODs

Competitive Play

- **Ranked Ladder** – Structured by seasons, featuring matchmaking tiers (Bronze to Grandmaster)

- **Tournaments** – Weekly community-hosted events, with occasional official developer-sponsored brackets

- **Clan Wars** – Team-based competitive mode with leaderboard tracking

Training Tools

- **Sandbox Mode** – Practice moves and setups with adjustable AI

- **Frame Viewer** – Analyze animation speed and move timing

- **Replay Analyzer** – Slow-motion replays with input overlays to refine technique

Social Media & Updates

Follow *Nubs!* on social platforms for patch alerts, event announcements, and community spotlights. Engaging here often rewards exclusive cosmetics or early access opportunities.